limpbizkit
results may vary

WWW.LIMPBIZKIT.COM

[TRA]NSCRIBED BY DANNY BEGELMAN

[MAN]AGERS: JEANNETTE DeLISA AND AARON STANG
[ ] MUSIC EDITOR: COLGAN BRYAN
[ ] ENGRAVER: W.R. MUSIC
[ ] TECHNICAL EDITOR: JACK ALLEN
[BO]OK ART LAYOUT: ERNESTO EBANKS
[AR]TWORK: © 2003 FLIP/INTERSCOPE RECORDS

limpbizkit

Contents

re-entry.....................................5
eat you alive........................8
gimme the mic...................16
underneath the gun.............23
down another day................34
almost over.........................43
build a bridge......................50
red light-green light............55
the only one........................61
let me down........................70
lonely world.........................77
phenomenon.......................84
creamer (radio is dead)........91
head for the barricade.........99
behind blue eyes.................104
drown.................................107

CA 90210 (310) 2

309041

Dr. DURDEN, TYLER

YONE, ABSOLUTELY MR/MS:
N ONCE DAILY---RESULTS MAY
AUSE EMOTIONAL REACTION QTY:

by:01/01/05
LIMPBIZKIT 1000%
left. please call

RE-ENTRY

All gtrs. in Drop D, down 1 1/2 steps:

⑥ = B   ③ = E
⑤ = F#   ② = G#
④ = B   ① = C#

Words and Music by
FRED DURST, JOHN OTTO
and SAMUEL RIVERS

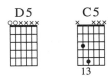

Spoken: "Step right up, step right up, everyone.
Whether you're good or bad, happy or sad;
Whether you're an emotional wreck or a
Blissful speck in this black hole of an existence we call life.
Step right up and witness something you will be sure to never forget.
Feast your ears on the most ferociously
Soothing waves of sonic communication to ever be created.
Built for you by the master. (Hey!) Built for you by the master.
(Hey! Shut up already! What is it?) What is it?
(Yeah, dawg, what is it?) What is it? (Dude, chill, man).
It is Limp Bizkit."

Moderately ♪ = 184

*Recording sounds a minor third lower then written.

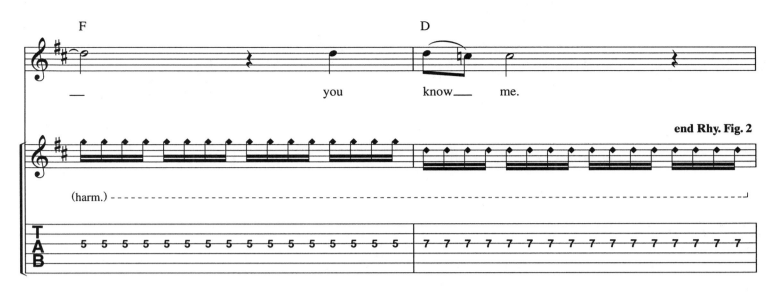

end Rhy. Fig. 2

(harm.)

you know___ me.

w/Rhy. Fig. 2 *(Elec. Gtrs. 1 & 2)*

All a - round___ the world___ we

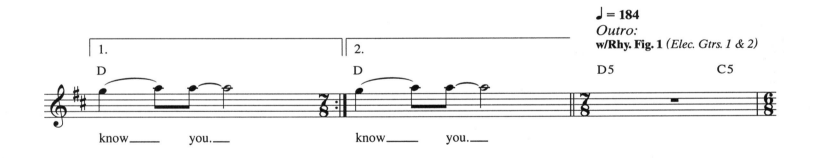

♩ = 184

Outro:
w/Rhy. Fig. 1 *(Elec. Gtrs. 1 & 2)*

1. know___ you.___

2. know___ you.___

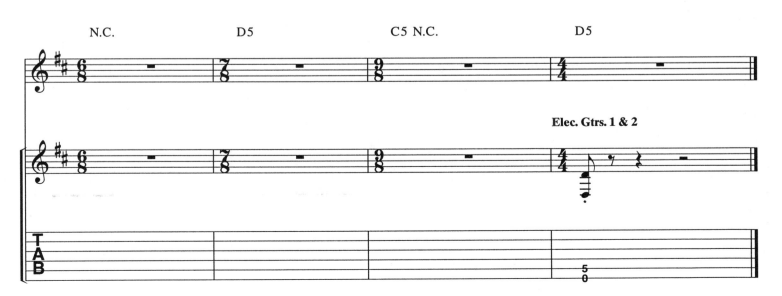

Elec. Gtrs. 1 & 2

EAT YOU ALIVE

Words and Music by
FRED DURST, JOHN OTTO,
SAMUEL RIVERS and MIKE SMITH

All gtrs. in Drop D, down 1 1/2 steps:

⑥ = B   ③ = E
⑤ = F#   ② = G#
④ = B   ① = C#

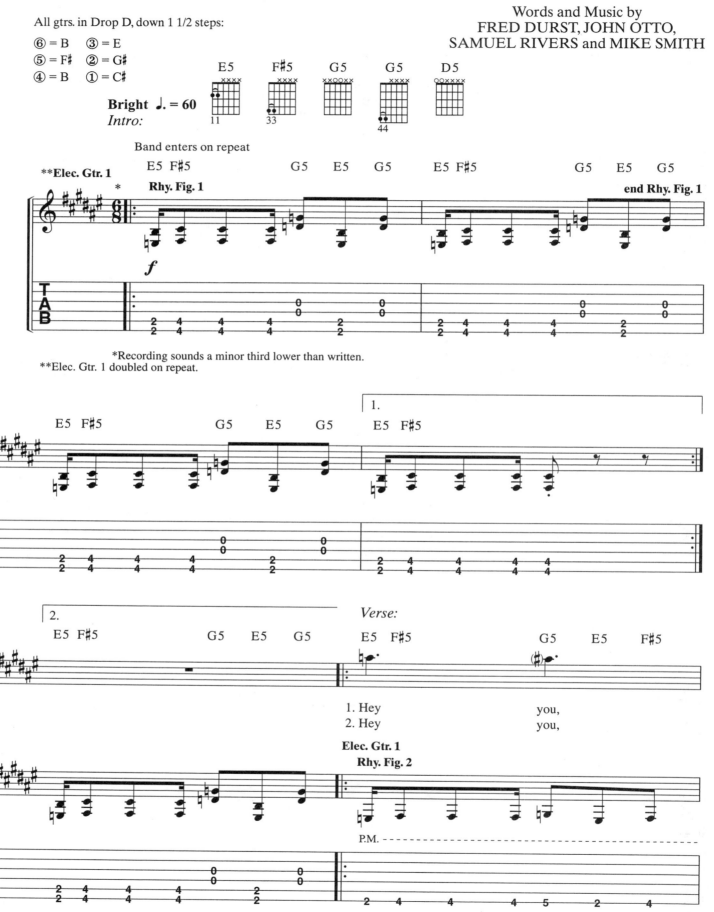

*Recording sounds a minor third lower than written.
**Elec. Gtr. 1 doubled on repeat.

1. Hey   you,
2. Hey   you,

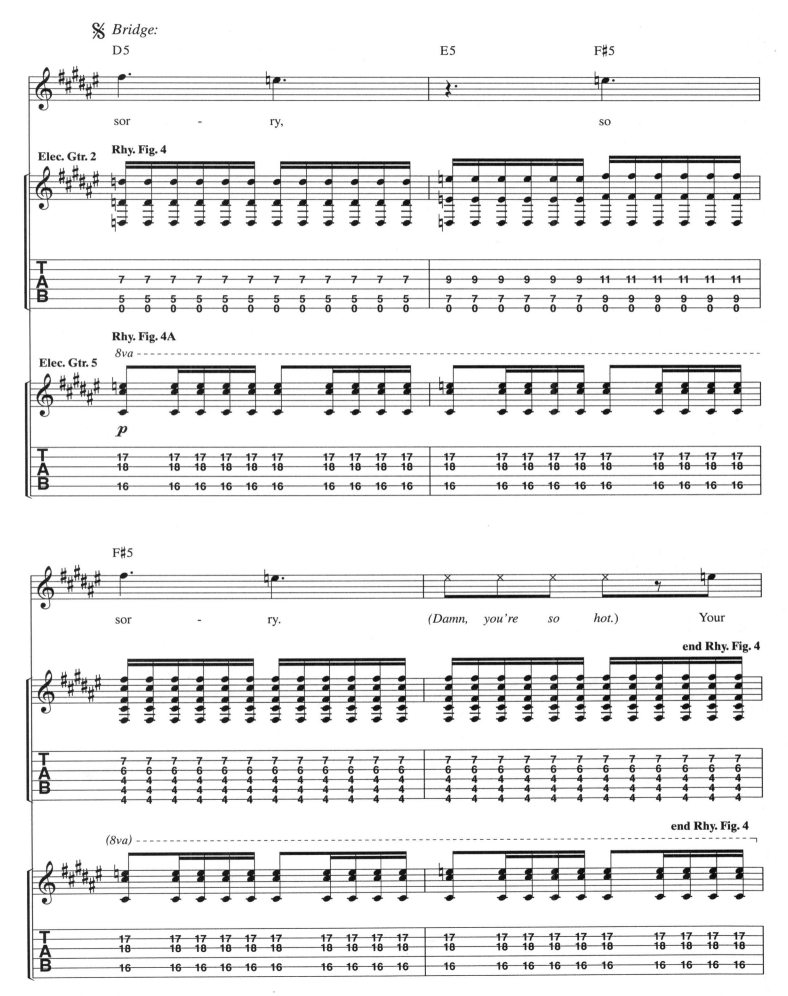

12

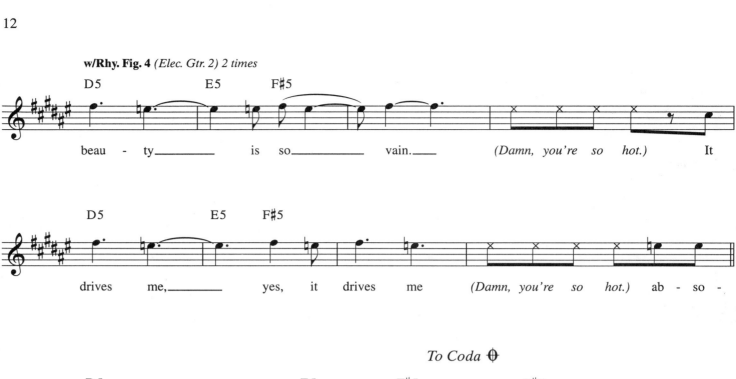

beau - ty____ is so____ vain.__ *(Damn, you're so hot.)* It

drives me,____ yes, it drives me *(Damn, you're so hot.)* ab - so -

To Coda ⊕

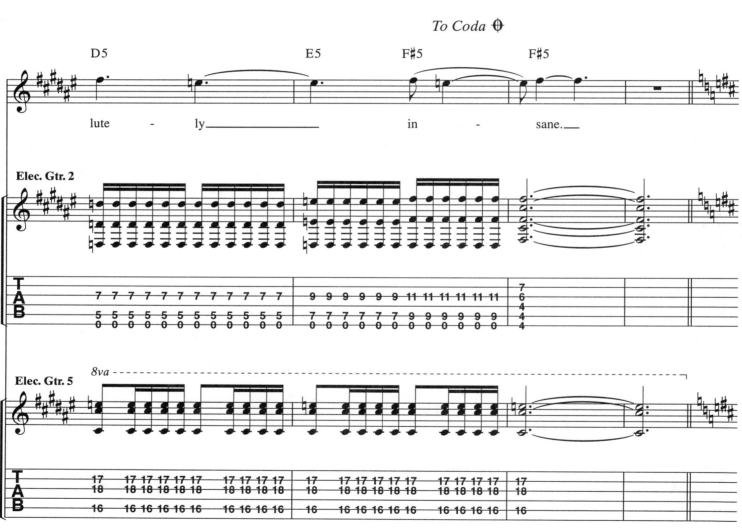

lute - ly_____ in - sane.__

Elec. Gtr. 2

Elec. Gtr. 5

Interlude:
(Elec. Gtrs. tacet 8 meas.)

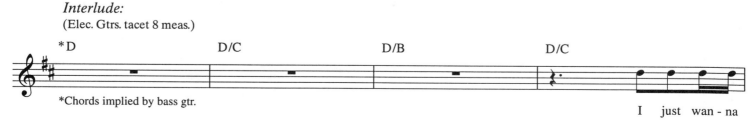

*Chords implied by bass gtr.

I just wan - na

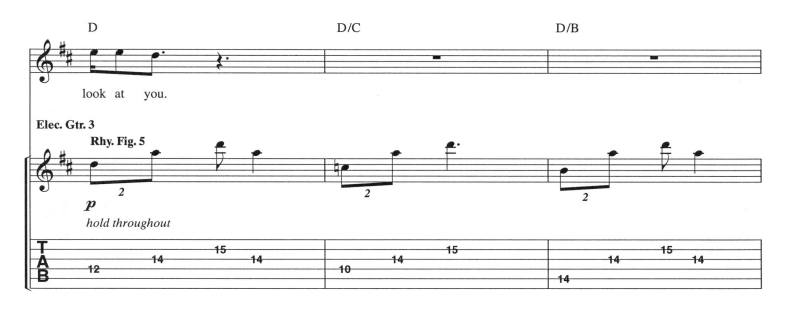

14

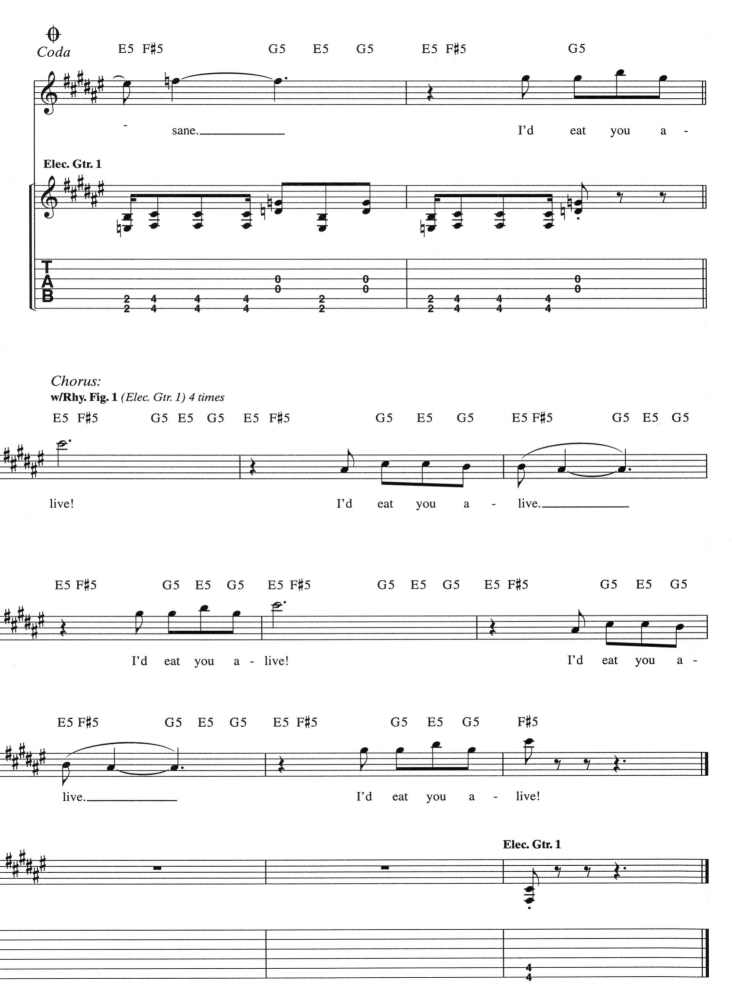

GIMME THE MIC

Words and Music by
FRED DURST, JOHN OTTO, SAMUEL RIVERS, MIKE SMITH,
ERIC BARRIER, WILLIAM GRIFFIN, ALAN E. GORRIE,
JAMES STUART, STEPHEN FERRONE, OWEN MCINTYRE,
ROGER BALL and MALCOLM DUNCAN

All gtrs. in Drop D, down 1 1/2 steps:

⑥ = B ③ = E
⑤ = F♯ ② = G♯
④ = B ① = C♯

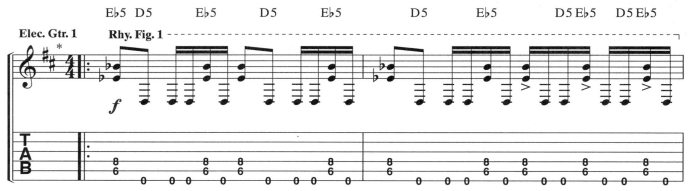

Moderately ♩ = 92
Intro:

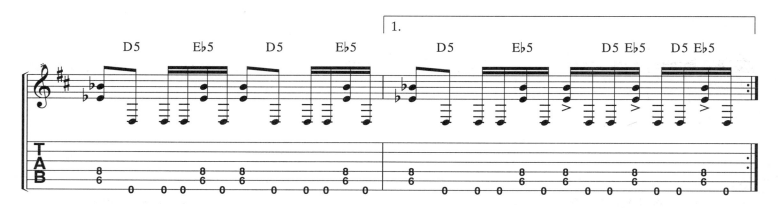

*Recording sounds a minor third lower than written.

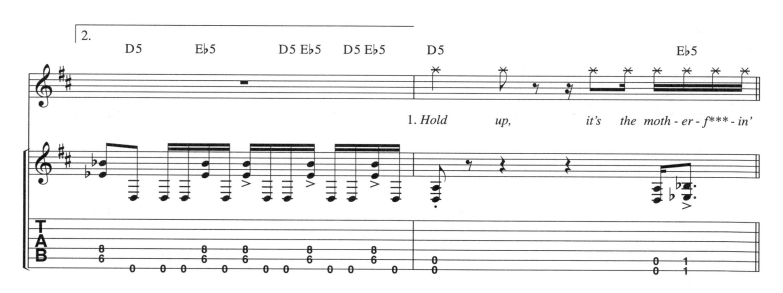

1. *Hold up, it's the moth-er-f***-in'*

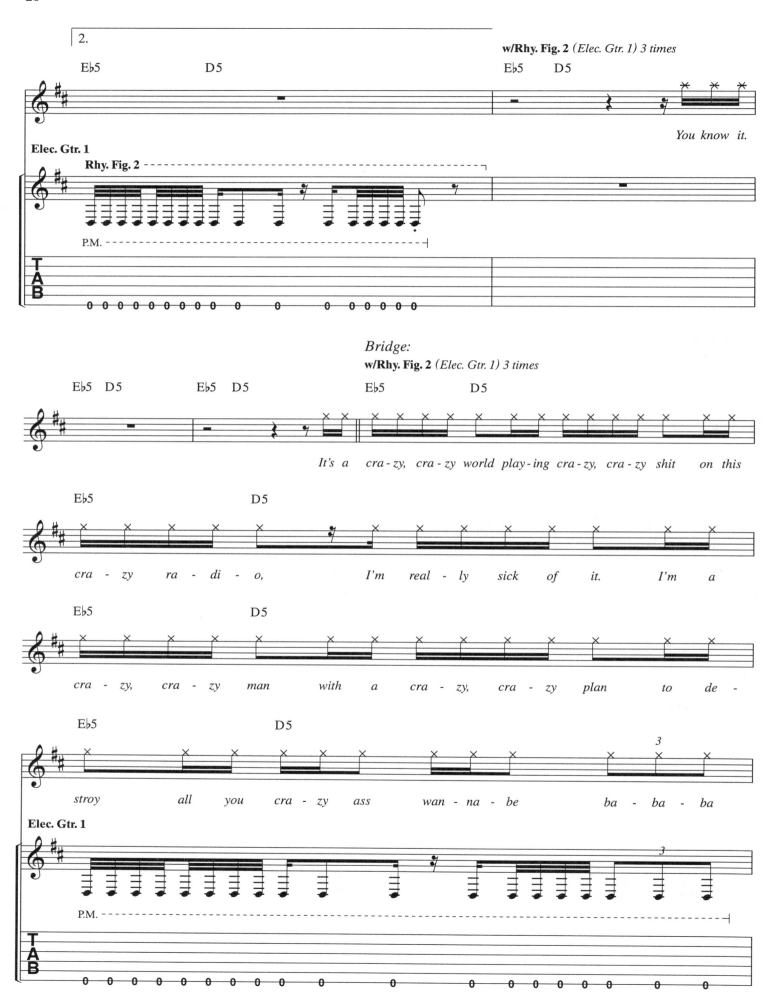

Chorus:
*C/E

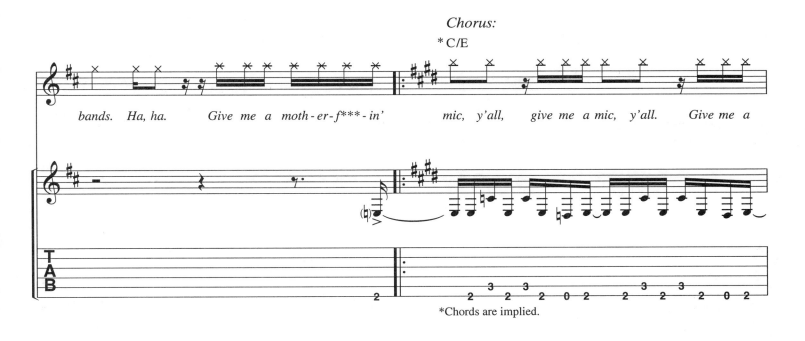

bands. Ha, ha.   Give me a moth-er-f***-in'   mic, y'all,   give me a mic, y'all.   Give me a

*Chords are implied.

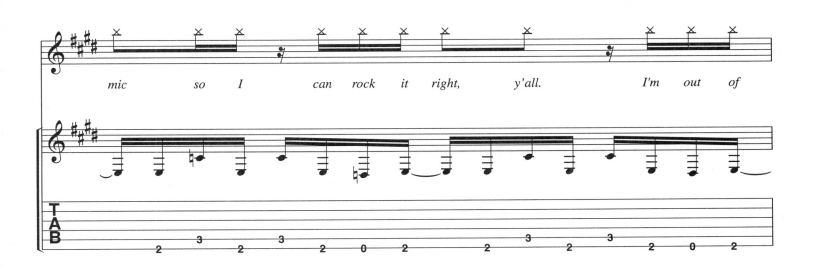

mic   so   I   can rock   it   right,   y'all.   I'm   out   of

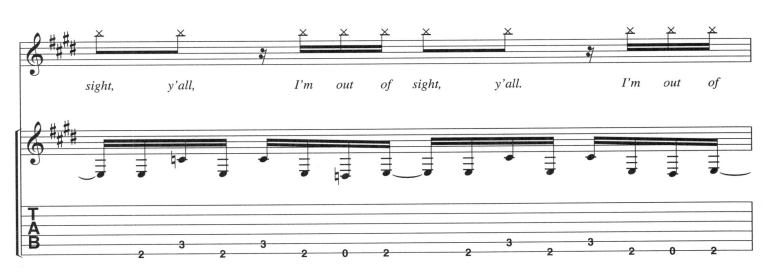

sight,   y'all,   I'm   out   of   sight,   y'all.   I'm   out   of

Gimme the Mic - 7 - 6
PGM0323

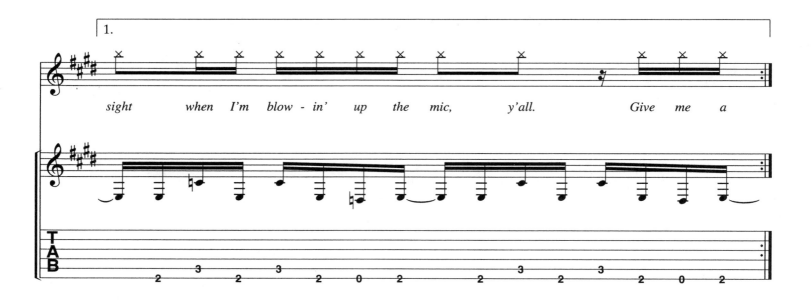

Verse 3:
Hold up, check out the mother-f***in' TV,
The same song, same bands everyday, f*** that.
I'll blow those motherf***er's away.
You wantin' to hear some heavy-ass metal that can
Penetrate deep in your eardrums?
Turn it up, motherf***er, turn it up, motherf***er.
Turn it up and step into a world that you've never seen,
When I'm feeling for a microphone I'm a microphone fiend.
(To Pre-chorus:)

UNDERNEATH THE GUN

Words and Music by
FRED DURST, JOHN OTTO,
SAMUEL RIVERS and MIKE SMITH

Elec. Gtr. 1 in Drop D, down 1 1/2 steps:
⑥ = B ③ = E
⑤ = F# ② = G#
④ = B ① = C#

Bright ♩ = **168**
Intro:

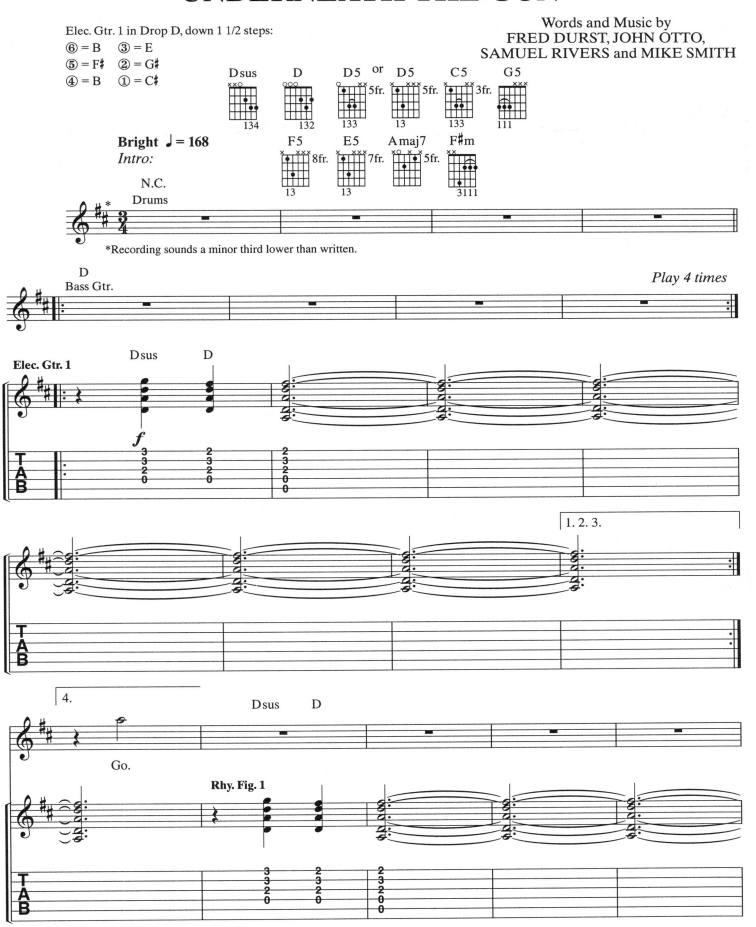

*Recording sounds a minor third lower than written.

Verse:
w/Rhy. Fig. 1 *(Elec. Gtr. 1) 4 times*

stare in - to space and hope we're not a - lone. Am I
los - ing my mind and I know there's no rem - e - dy.

search - ing for some - thing that's bet - ter than home.
Think I'm a fail - ure who's liv - ing on mem - o - ries.

I've been work - ing so hard._____
I've been work - ing so hard._____

Stress is tre - men - dous and pres - sure is end - less. No
Lone - li - ness can't be cured from no med - i - cine.

one on this plan - et like me to be friends with.
Look to the stars so they'll strength - en my head a - gain.

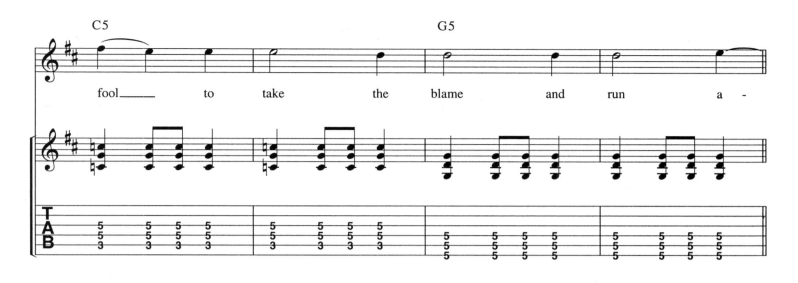

fool_____ to take the blame and run a-

Guitar Solo:

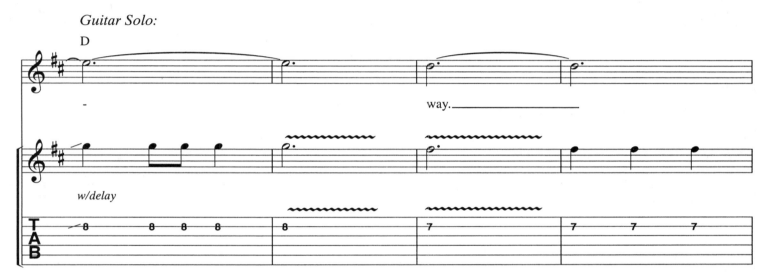

- way._____

w/delay

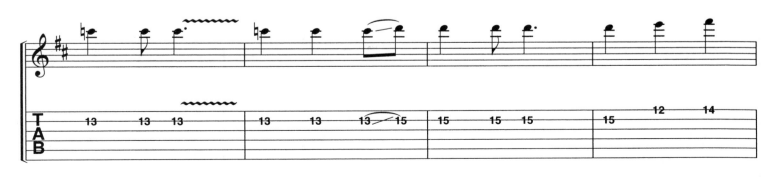

28

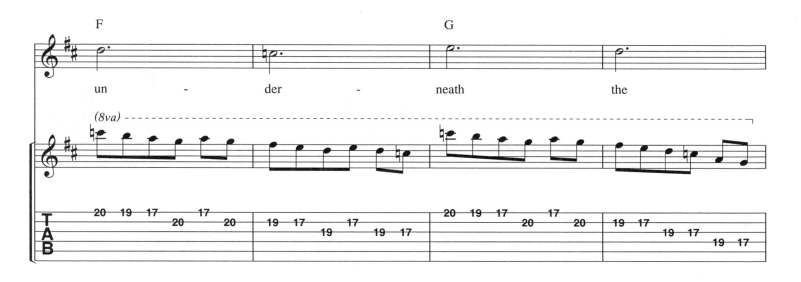

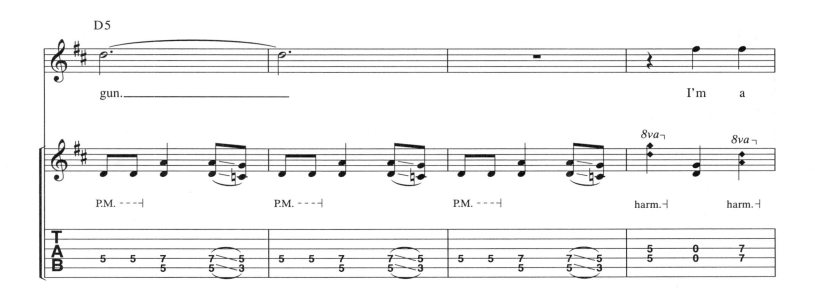

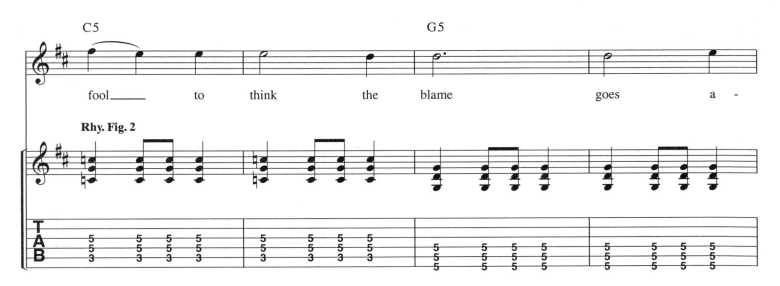

Bridge 1:

w/Rhy. Fig. 3 *(Elec. Gtr. 1) 7 times*

Some - times I beat up my -

self. I block my own

way. I cloud all my

thoughts, please go a - way. Oh, nev - er

mind, please, I'm check - in'

out now. And won't ev - er

come back now that my

life does - n't ex - ist. Yeah, you're

Elec. Gtr. 1

P.M.

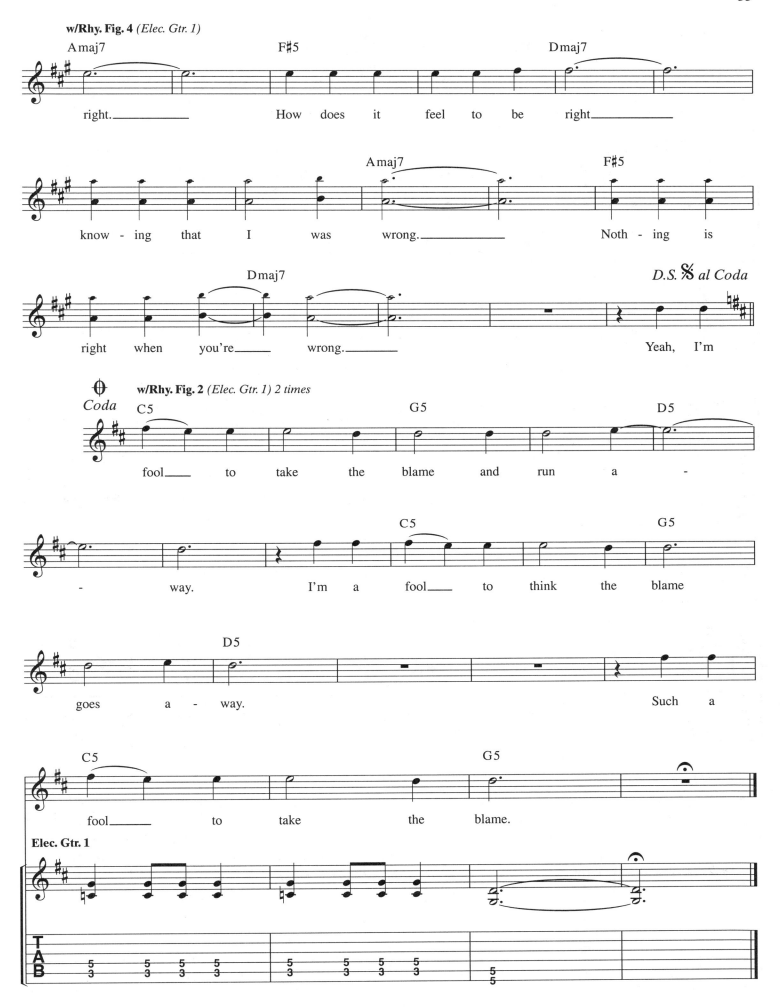

DOWN ANOTHER DAY

All gtrs. in Drop D, down 1 1/2 steps:

⑥ = B　③ = E
⑤ = F♯　② = G♯
④ = B　① = C♯

Words and Music by
FRED DURST, JOHN OTTO
and SAMUEL RIVERS

Moderately ♩ = 112
(Half-time feel)
Intro:

A5　C5　D5　E5　G5　A5　C5　D5　E5

Elec. Gtr. 1

Rhy. Fig. 1 -

mf

Recording sounds a minor third lower than written.

𝄋 Verse:

w/Rhy. Fig. 1 *(Elec. Gtr. 1) 3 times*
w/Fill 1 *(Elec. Gtr. 5) 2 times, 3rd time only*

A5　C5　D5　E5　G5　A5　C5　D5　E5

1. The end is near,___ my sum-mer days.___ All great___ things go a-way.___

day.

2. 3. *See additional lyrics*

Elec. Gtr. 2

Rhy. Fig. 2　　　　　　　　　　　　　　　**end Rhy. Fig. 2**

8va -

p

Fill 1
Elec. Gtr. 5

8va -

p

Down Another Day - 9 - 1

PGM0323

And when she's gold - en,___ the o - cean...___

___)

(will nev - er let you down.___)

o - cean...___

Elec. Gtr. 3

Acous. Gtr.

Outro:
w/Fill 3 *(Elec. Gtr. 7) 4 times*

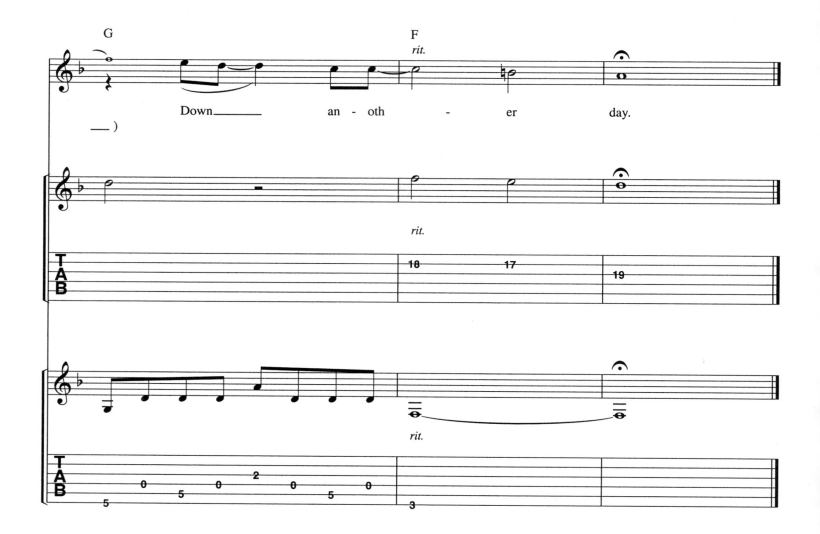

Verse 2:
Oh, the winter I adore.
Summer's gone for ever more.
Some day she'll come back to me.
Season's change to set me free
Down another day.
(To Chorus:)

Verse 3:
The end is near, my winter fling.
Change is melting everything.
Now it's time to sink below,
Season comes, season goes.
Down another day.
Down another day.
(To Chorus:)

Almost Over

Words and Music by
FRED DURST, JOHN OTTO,
SAMUEL RIVERS and MIKE SMITH

minds.
minds.
(Ah, ah, ah, ah, ah, ah, ah, ah.)

2. Learn   how to
4. Got treat-ed like a

Verses 2 & 4:
Rhy. Fig. 1 (Elec. Gtr. 2) 4 times

D5

lose as an old-er man.   Sang a lot of blues as an old-er man.   But I saw it all
chump as an old-er man.   Mix-in' rock with the funk as an old-er man.   Learned what a girl

* Elec. Gtr. 2 w/dist.

G5   F5

through as an old-er man.   Put to-geth-er my crew as an old-er man.   Felt a lot of
was as an old-er man.   Now I know how to love as an old-er man.   But I'm still a big

D5

pain as an old-er man.   I es-tab-lished my name as an old-er man.   Peo-ple piss in my
kid as an old-er man.   And I'd much rath-er give as an old-er man.   Still I'm sing-ing in the

G5   F5

game as an old-er man.   Ain't noth-in' gon-na change as an old-er man.
rain as an old-er man.   Ain't noth-in' gon-na change as an old-er man.   It's time to blow their

Pre-chorus:

D5   F5   G5

minds now, ba-by.   It's time to blow their minds now, ba-by.   I'm on my

Elec. Gtr. 3

f

T
A
B

Almost Over - 7 - 2
PGM0323

* Chords implied by bass gtr.

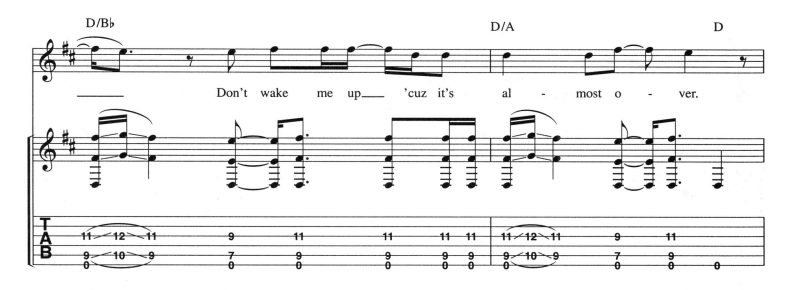

Don't wake me up___ 'cuz it's al - most o - ver.

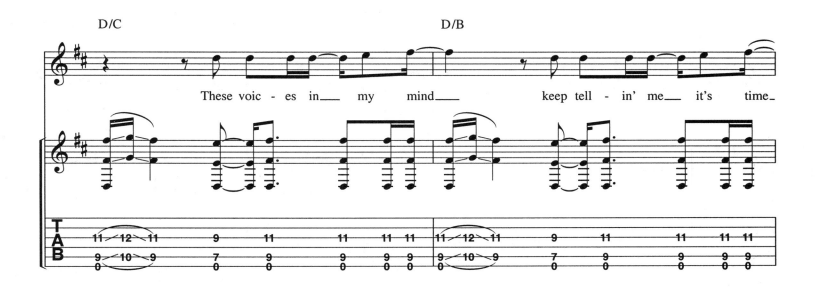

These voic - es in___ my mind___ keep tell - in' me___ it's time___

To Coda ✛

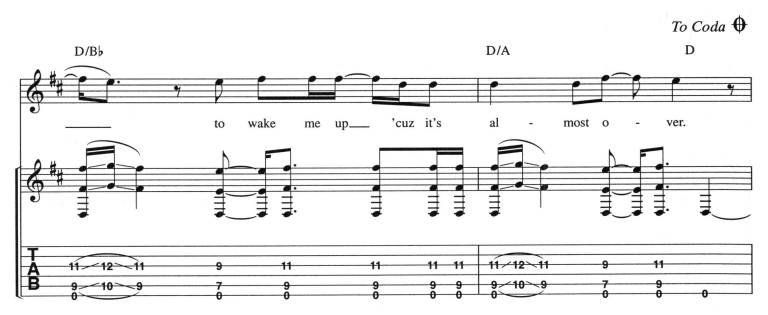

___ to wake me up___ 'cuz it's al - most o - ver.

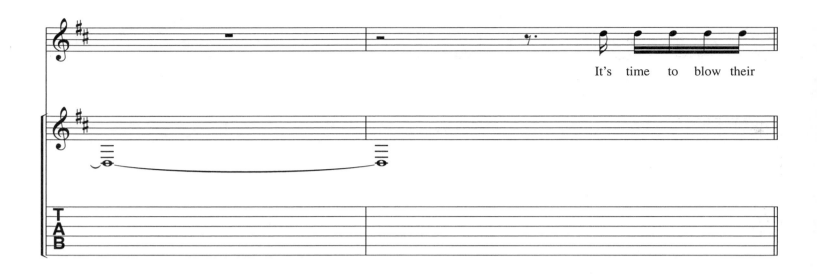

It's time to blow their

Pre-chorus:

Elec. Gtr. 3 tacet

D5   F5   G5

minds now, ba - by.   It's time to blow their minds now, ba - by.   I'm on my

F5

grind now, ba - by.   Y'all know it's my time now, ba - by.   It's time to blow their

D5   F5   G5

minds now, ba - by.   It's time to blow their minds now, ba - by.   I'm on my

Elec. Gtr. 3

BUILD A BRIDGE

All gtrs. in Drop D, down 1 1/2 steps:
⑥ = B   ③ = E
⑤ = F#   ② = G#
④ = B   ① = C#

Words and Music by
FRED DURST, JOHN OTTO
and SAMUEL RIVERS

*Recording sounds a minor third lower than written.

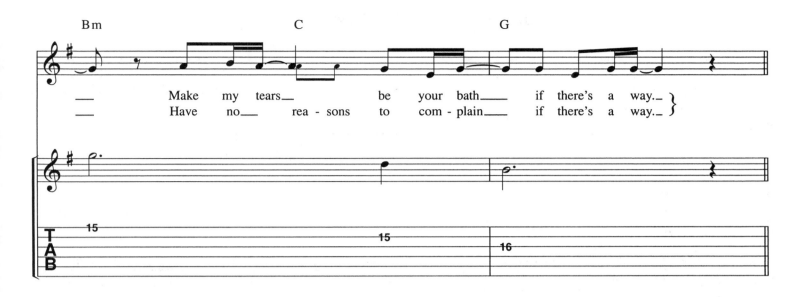

Make my tears__ be your bath__ if there's a way.__
Have no__ rea - sons to com - plain__ if there's a way.__

Pre-chorus:

On - ly if you'll take a ride.

Acous. Gtr.

hold throughout

Go with me to the oth - er side.

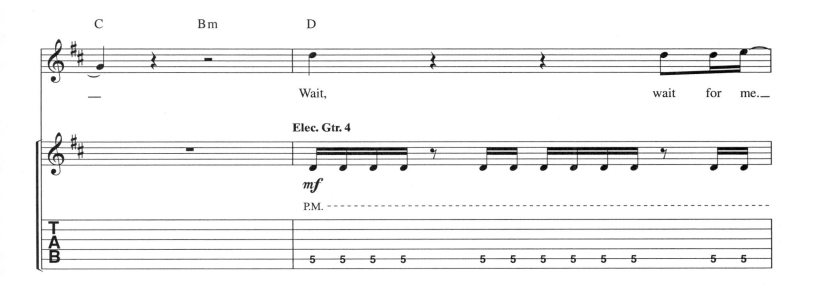

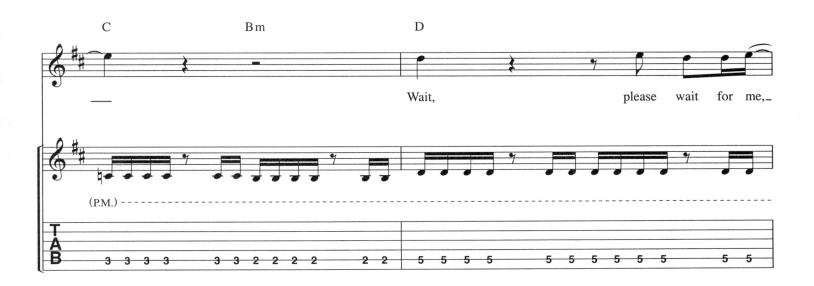

54

crum - ble down,
(Gon - na crum - ble down.)
I'll keep build - ing till you

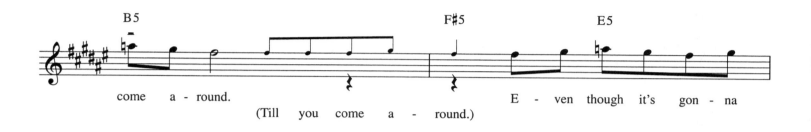

come a - round.
(Till you come a - round.)
E - ven though it's gon - na

D.S. % al Coda

fall a - part and break my heart,
(Gon - na fall a - part.)
I'll keep build - ing till I die.

Coda

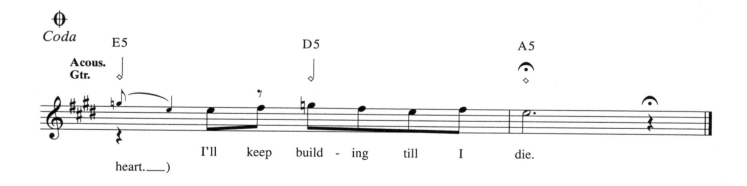

heart.___)
I'll keep build - ing till I die.

RED LIGHT - GREEN LIGHT

All gtrs. in Drop D, down 1 1/2 steps:

⑥ = B   ③ = E
⑤ = F♯   ② = G♯
④ = B   ① = C♯

Words and Music by
FRED DURST, LEOR DIMANT
and CALVIN BROADUS

Moderately ♩ = 92

Intro:

"Ladies and gentlemen, Limp Bizkit and Snoop Dog."

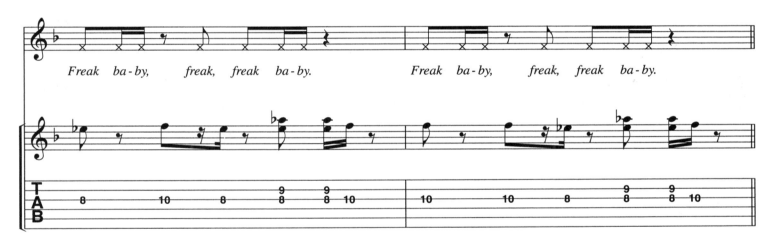

*Recording sounds a minor third lower then written.

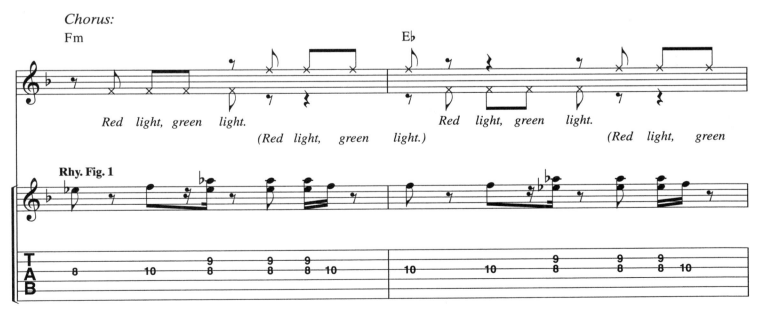

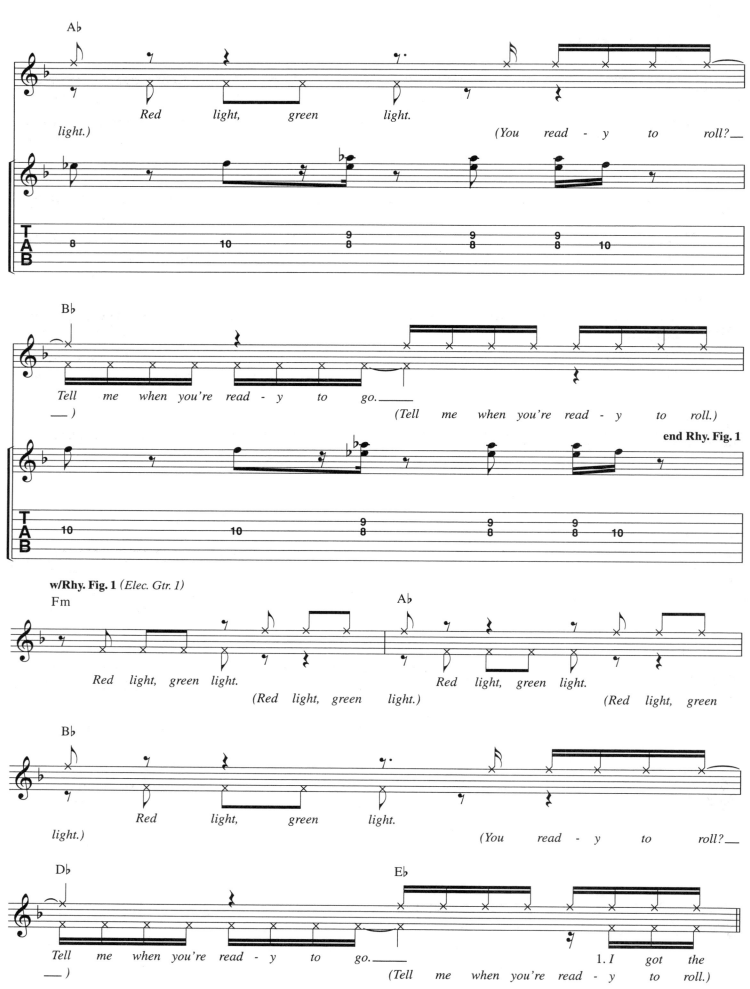

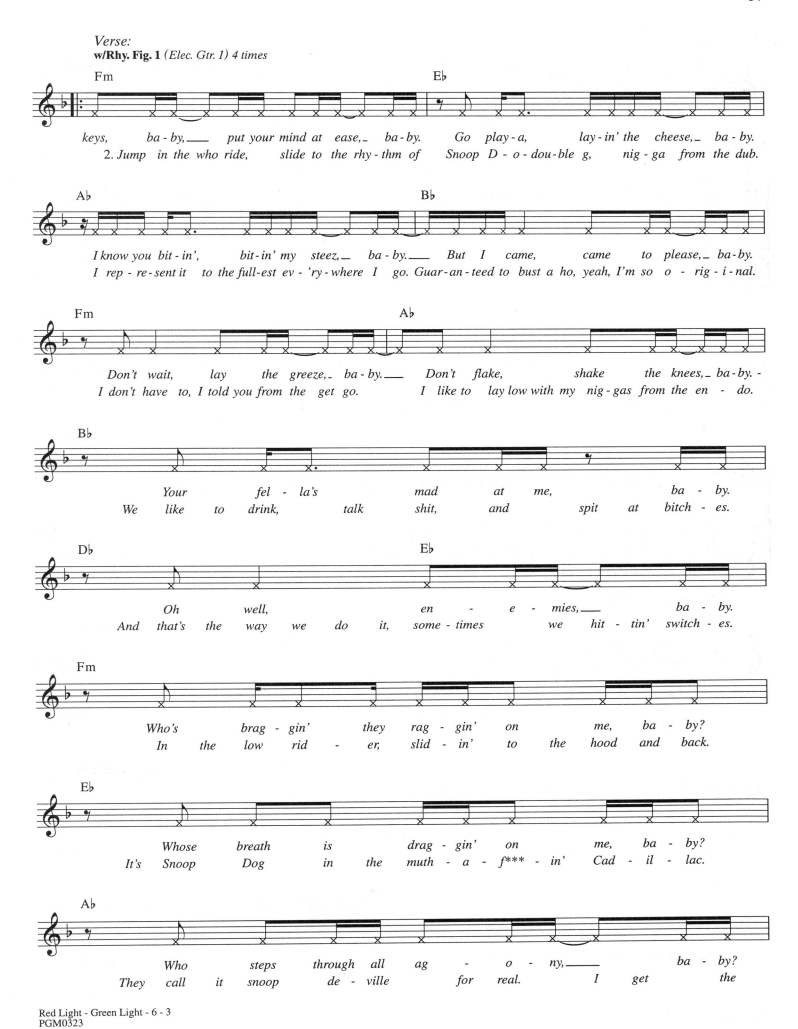

60

Fm

Freak ba - by,   freak, freak ba - by.   *Freak ba - by,   freak, freak ba - by.*

(Tell me when you're read - y   to roll.)

Bb   **Db**   **Eb**   **To Coda** ✛

Freak ba - by,   freak, freak ba - by.   Tell me when you're read - y to go.

(Tell me when you're read - y to roll.)

Elec. Gtr. tacet

N.C.

Look who's   talk - in' it up,___ ba - by.   One more   chalk - in' it up,___ ba - by.

Star maps   stalk - in' it up,___ ba - by.   My dog's   bark - in' it up,___ ba - by.

w/Rhy. Fig. 1 *(Elec. Gtr. 1)*

Fm   **Ab**

Who'd a thought I'd be lay - in' it down,_ ba - by?   Who'd a thought I'd be turn - in' your frown,_ ba - by?

Bb   **Db**   **Eb**   **D.S.** ✵ **al Coda**

Nev - er know a - bout things these days,   ba - by,   till your cell - phone rings and it's me, ba - by.

✛
Coda **Fm**

Elec. Gtr. 1 tacet

Freak ba - by,   freak, freak ba - by.   Freak ba - by,   freak, freak   ba - by.

(Tell me when you're read - y to roll.)

N.C.

Freak ba - by,   freak, freak ba - by.   Tell me when you're read - y to go.

THE ONLY ONE

All gtrs. in Drop D, down 1 1/2 steps:

⑥ = B ③ = E
⑤ = F# ② = G#
④ = B ① = C#

Words and Music by
FRED DURST, JOHN OTTO,
SAMUEL RIVERS and MIKE SMITH

Moderately ♩ = 76

Intro:

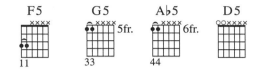

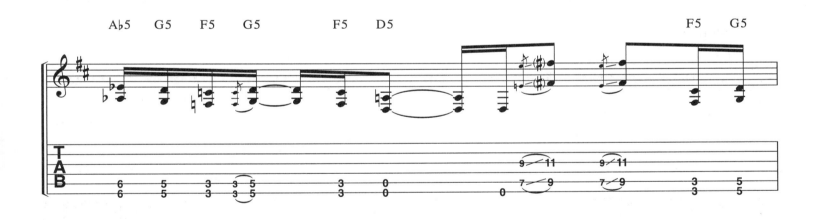

*Recording sounds a minor third lower than written.

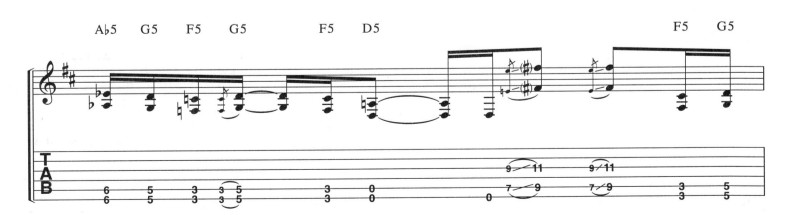

The Only One - 9 - 1
PGM0323

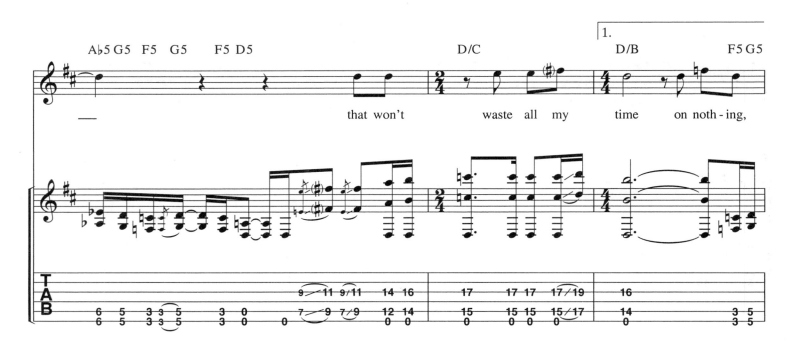

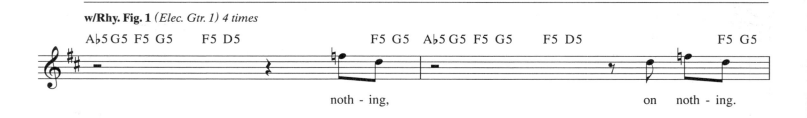

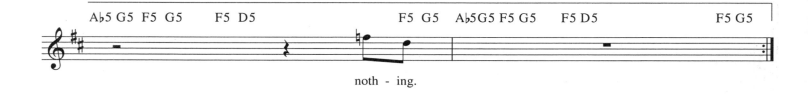

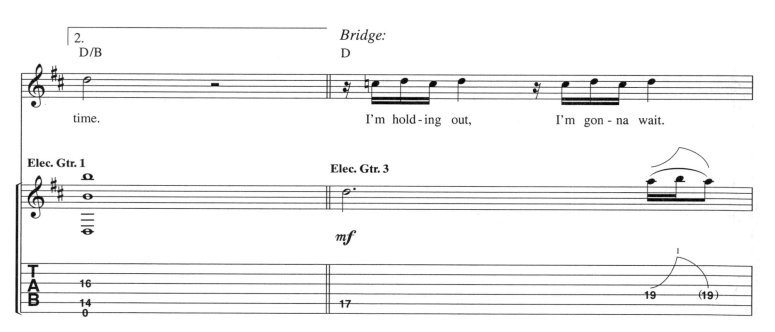

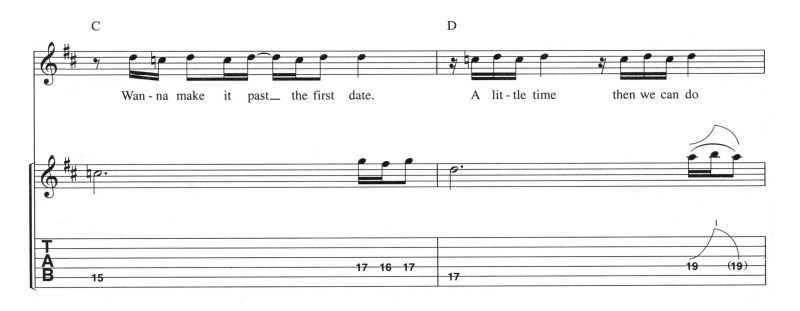

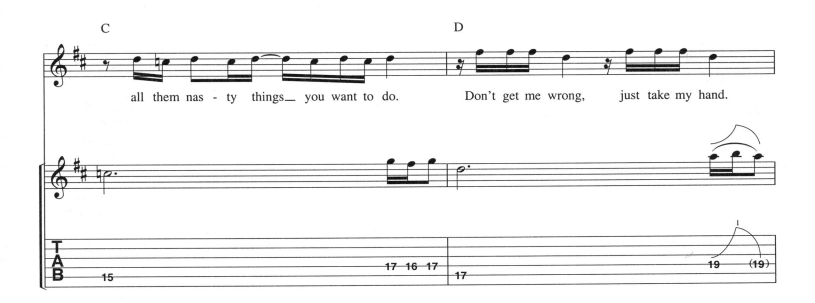

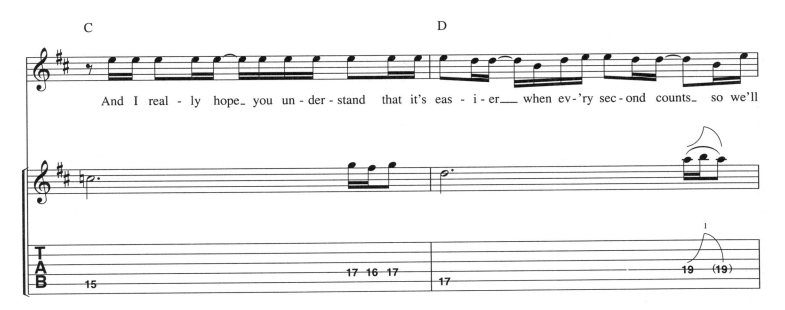

just have to wait. It's real - ly

*Chords implied by bass gtr.

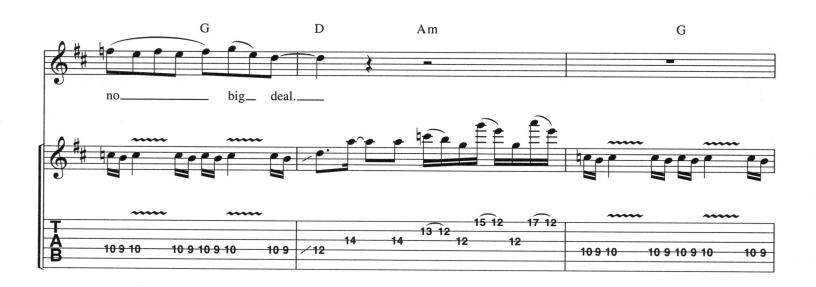

no_____ big__ deal.____

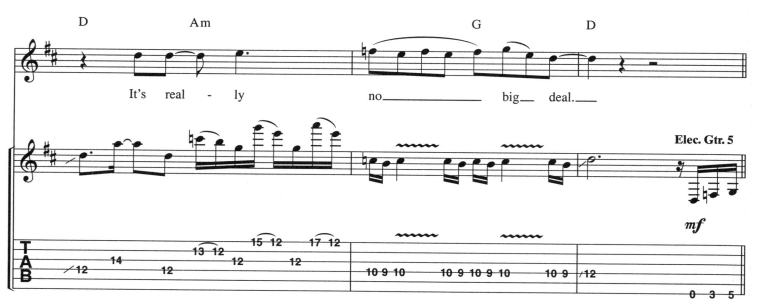

It's real - ly no_____ big__ deal.____

Verse 3:

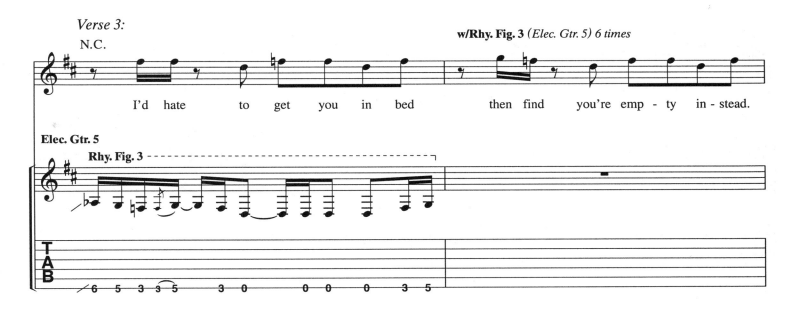

I'd hate to get you in bed then find you're emp - ty in - stead.

No need_ to knock an - oth - er home run out_ 'cause that's a no go._

And I hate_ to be so filth - y if we_ were not meant to be.

No need_ to knock an - oth - er home run out._ See I'm

Chorus:

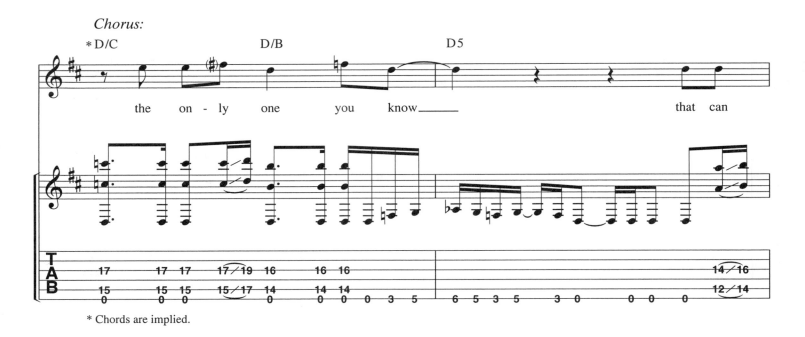

* Chords are implied.

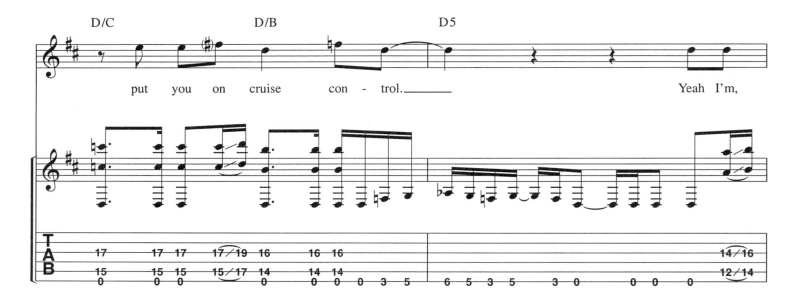

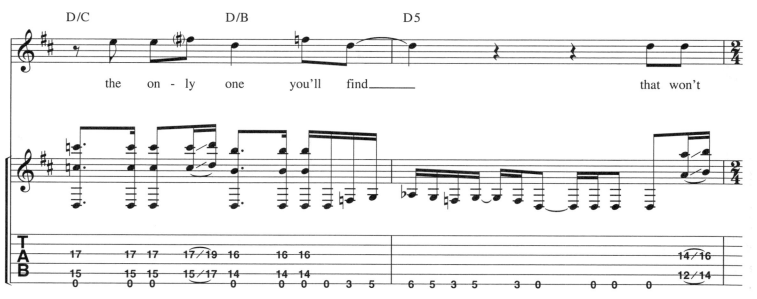

LET ME DOWN

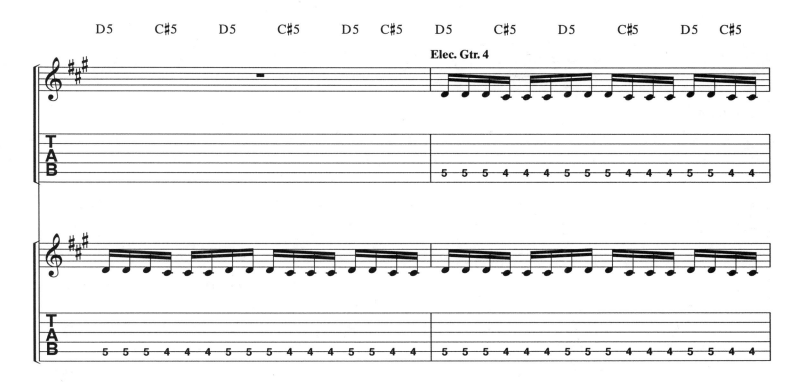

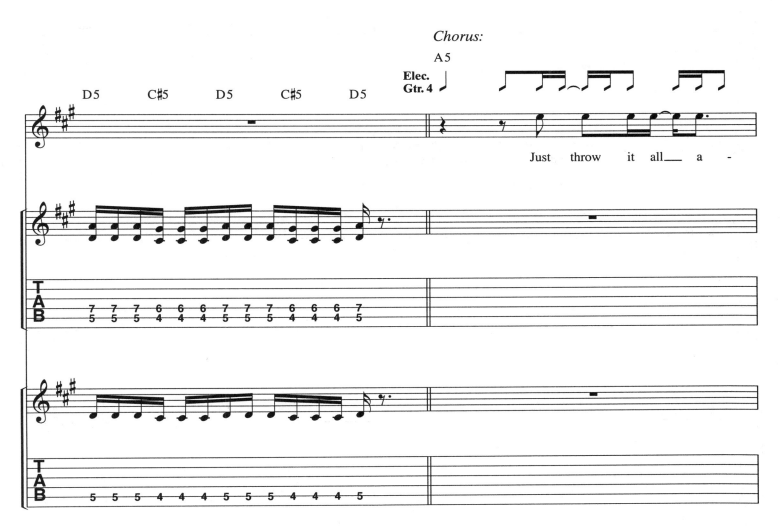

Let Me Down - 7 - 6
PGM0323

76

LONELY WORLD

Words and Music by
FRED DURST, JOHN OTTO,
SAMUEL RIVERS and MIKE SMITH

All gtrs. in Drop D, down 1 1/2 steps:

⑥ = B   ③ = E
⑤ = F#   ② = G#
④ = B   ① = C#

Moderately ♩ = 92

Intro:

Recording sounds a minor third lower than written.

w/Rhy. Fig. 1 *(Bass Gtr.)*

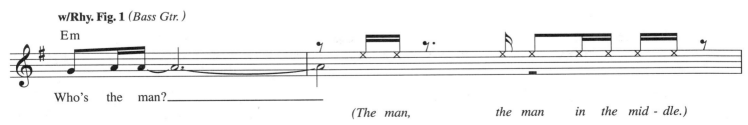

Who's the man?_____

(The man,   the man   in   the mid-dle.)

Lonely World - 7 - 1
PGM0323

78

try in - side a lone - ly world, no one can hear me when I cry in - side a lone - ly world.

I'll nev - er know the rea - sons why in - side a lone - ly world, such a lone - ly world...

w/Rhy. Fig. 2 *(Elec. Gtr. 1) 4 times*

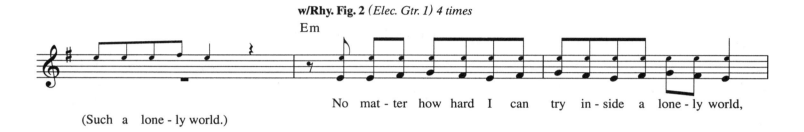

No mat - ter how hard I can try in - side a lone - ly world,

(Such a lone - ly world.)

no one can hear me when I cry in - side a lone - ly world. I'll nev - er know the rea - sons

D.S. 𝄋 *al Coda*

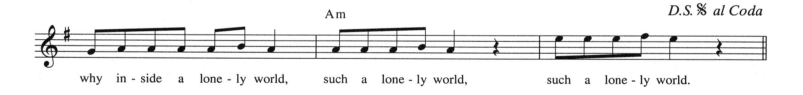

why in - side a lone - ly world, such a lone - ly world, such a lone - ly world.

Outro:
w/Rhy. Fig. 1 *(Bass Gtr.) 2 times*

Coda

Such a lone - ly world. Who's the man?

Elec. Gtr. 2

PHENOMENON

All gtrs. in Drop D, down 1 1/2 steps:

⑥ = B   ③ = E
⑤ = F♯   ② = G♯
④ = B   ① = C♯

A5   G5   B♭5   C5
7fr. 5fr. 8fr. 3fr.

Words and Music by
FRED DURST, JOHN OTTO, SAMUEL RIVERS,
LEOR DIMANT, GEORGE CLINTON, ARTHUR BAKER,
JOHN ROBIE, SYLVIA ROBINSON, ROBERT ALLEN,
AFRIKA BAMBAATA, ELLIS WILLIAMS, MELVIN GLOVER,
ERIC T. SADLER, JAMES HENRY BOXLEY,
EMIL SCHULT, RALF HUTTER and CARLTON RIDENHOUR

Moderately ♩ = 92
Intro:

D5

Elec. Gtr. 1
Rhy. Fig. 1 - - - - - - - - - - - - - - -

Are you

Recording sounds a minor third lower than written.

w/Rhy. Fig. 1 *(Elec. Gtr. 1) 3 times*

Band enters
Elec. Gtr. 1 dbld.

read - y?   *Ooh,_____ c - 'mon.*

𝄋 **Verse:**

Ddim7

w/Rhy. Fig. 2 *(Elec. Gtr. 2) 7 times*

1. *Ain't it fun-ny how time flies.* (Huh?)   *Out of sight,__ out of mind.* (Yeah, right.)
2. *Ain't it fun-ny how time flies.* (Huh?)   *Chit,__ chat-ter,__ that shit don't mat-ter.__*
3. *See additional lyrics*

Elec. Gtr. 2
Rhy. Fig. 2 - - - - - - - - - - - - - - - - - -

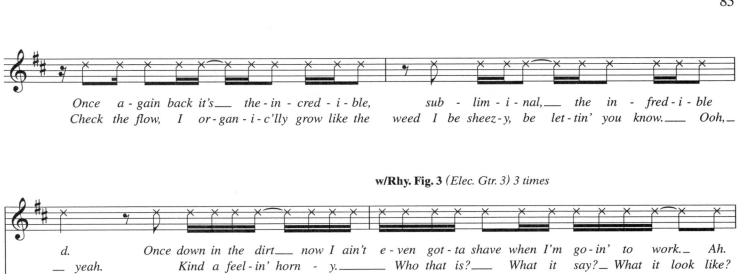

Once a-gain back it's__ the in-cred-i-ble, sub-lim-i-nal,__ the in-fred-i-ble
Check the flow, I or-gan-i-c'lly grow like the weed I be sheez-y, be let-tin' you know.__ Ooh,

w/**Rhy. Fig. 3** *(Elec. Gtr. 3) 3 times*

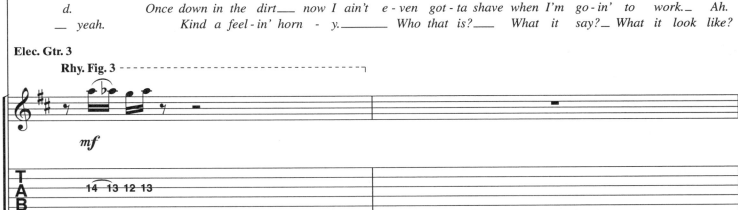

d. Once down in the dirt__ now I ain't e-ven got-ta shave when I'm go-in' to work.__ Ah.
__ yeah. Kind a feel-in' horn - y._____ Who that is?__ What it say?__ What it look like?

Elec. Gtr. 3

Rhy. Fig. 3

mf

1.

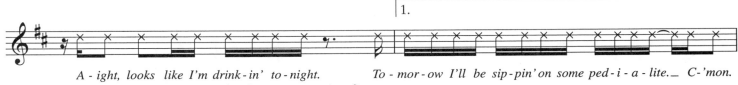

A - ight, looks like I'm drink-in' to-night. To - mor-ow I'll be sip-pin' on some ped-i-a-lite.__ C-'mon.
Twen - ty eyes in my head,_____ mis - fit.

w/**Rhy. Fig. 1** *(Elec. Gtr. 4) 2 times*

D5

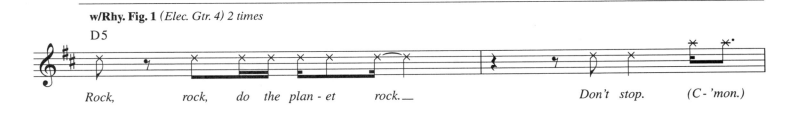

Rock, rock, do the plan - et rock.__ Don't stop. (C - 'mon.)

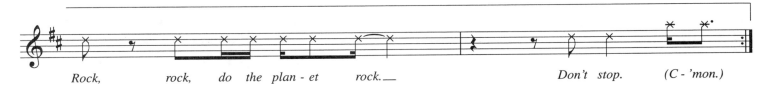

Rock, rock, do the plan - et rock.__ Don't stop. (C - 'mon.)

2. *To Next Strain (To Chorus:)* **3.**

Ddim7 **Ddim7**

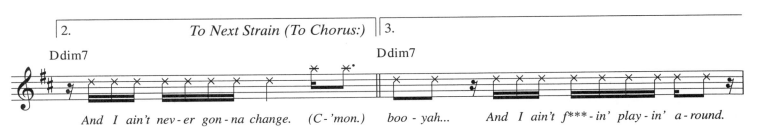

And I ain't nev-er gon-na change. (C-'mon.) boo - yah... And I ain't f***-in' play-in' a-round.

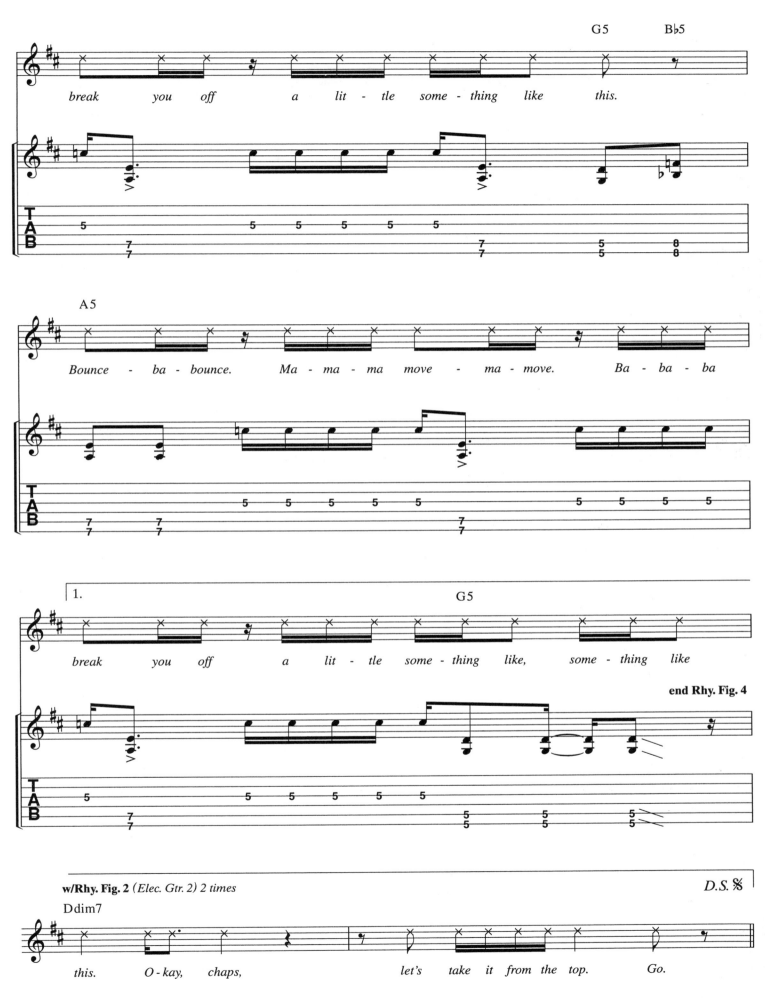

break you off a lit - tle some - thing like this.

Bounce - ba - bounce. Ma - ma - ma move - ma - move. Ba - ba - ba

1.

break you off a lit - tle some - thing like, some - thing like

end Rhy. Fig. 4

w/Rhy. Fig. 2 *(Elec. Gtr. 2) 2 times*

D.S. %

Ddim7

this. O - kay, chaps, let's take it from the top. Go.

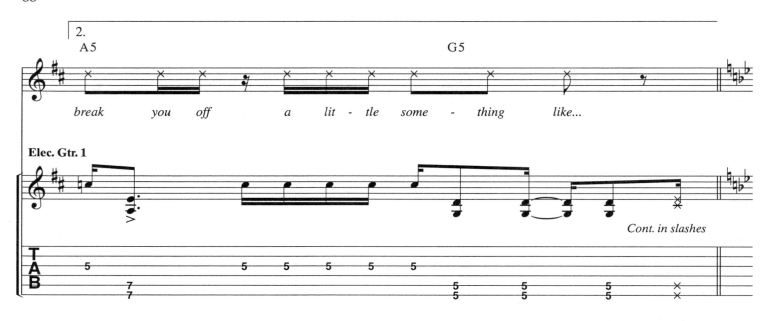

Bridge:

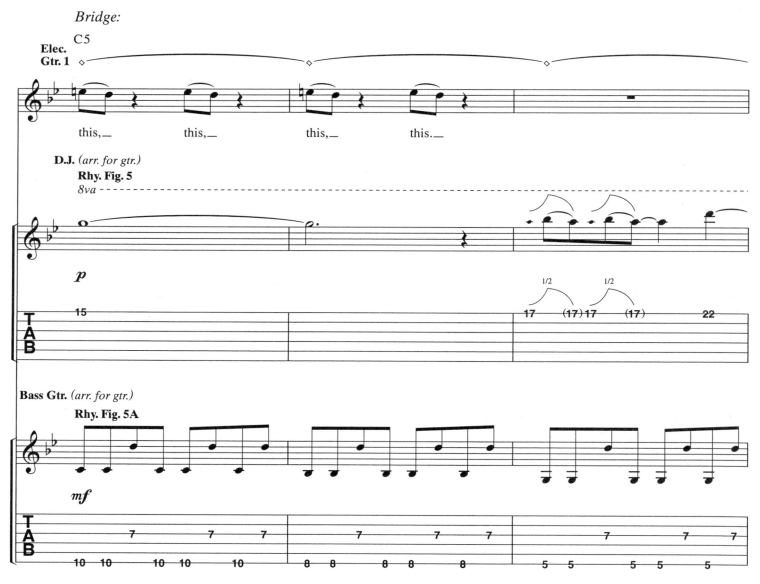

90

Interlude:

D5

I'd turn it on up. (Oh yeah.—) And I'd shut it on up. (Oh yeah.—)

Elec. Gtr. 1

Rhy. Fig. 6

w/Rhy. Fig. 6 *(Elec. Gtr. 1) 3 times*

And I'd bring that beat back. Aigh't,— then bring it on back. Go.

—) (Oh yeah.—)

Yeah. Bring that beat back. I'm a make ya

(I say what?)

Outro:

w/Rhy. Fig. 4 *(Elec. Gtr. 1) 1st 2 meas. only, 2 times*

A5   G5 B♭5

bounce - ba - bounce. Ma - ma - ma move - ma - move. Ba - ba - ba break you off a lit - tle some - thing like this.

A5   G5 B♭5

Bounce - ba - bounce. Ma - ma - ma move - ma - move. Ba - ba - ba break you off a lit - tle some - thing like this.

w/Rhy. Fig. 4 *(Elec. Gtr. 1)*

A5   G5 B♭5 A5   G5

Yeah. Yeah. A lit - tle some - thing like this. Yeah. Yeah. It's Limp Biz - kit, ba - by.

Verse 3:
Spoken:
All you Hollywood rockstars,
Hollywood ass, wishin' you had big cash.
Rollin' like you're pimpin,
But you ain't really got shit goin'.
'Cuz you ain't limpin' like the Bizkit,
You're just sittin' on the sidelines.
You just fake, kid, if there's a title, then I'll take it.
Who-yah, hit ya with the boo-yah...
And I ain't f***in' playin' around.
(To Chorus:)

CREAMER
(Radio Is Dead)

Words and Music by
FRED DURST, JOHN OTTO
and SAMUEL RIVERS

All gtrs. in Drop D, down 1 1/2 steps:

⑥ = B   ③ = E
⑤ = F♯   ② = G♯
④ = B   ① = C♯

Moderately ♩ = 98
Intro:

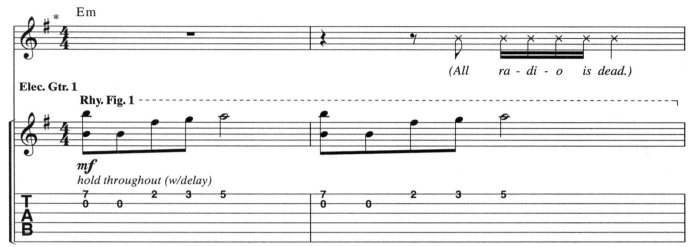

Recording sounds a minor third lower than written.

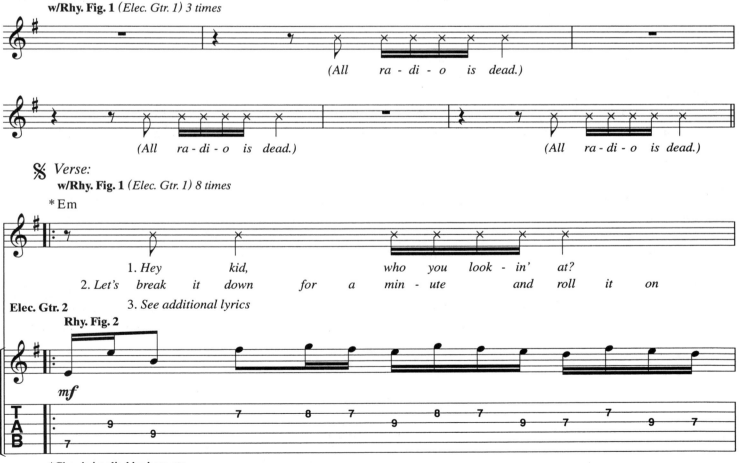

Chords implied by bass gtr.

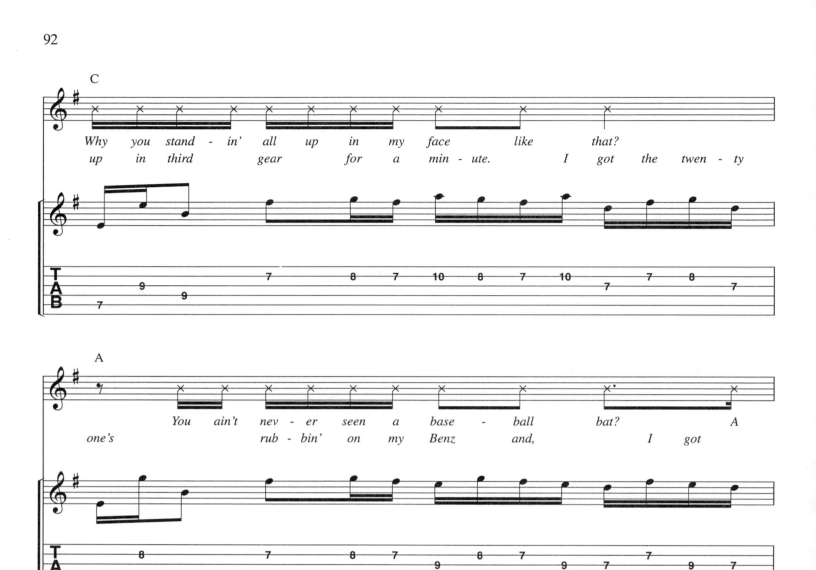

w/Rhy. Fig. 2 (Elec. Gtr. 2) 3 times

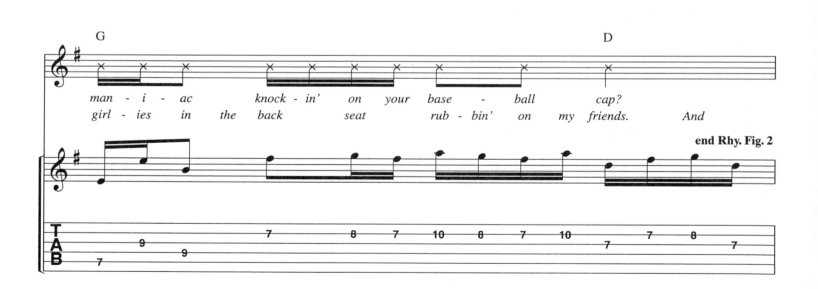

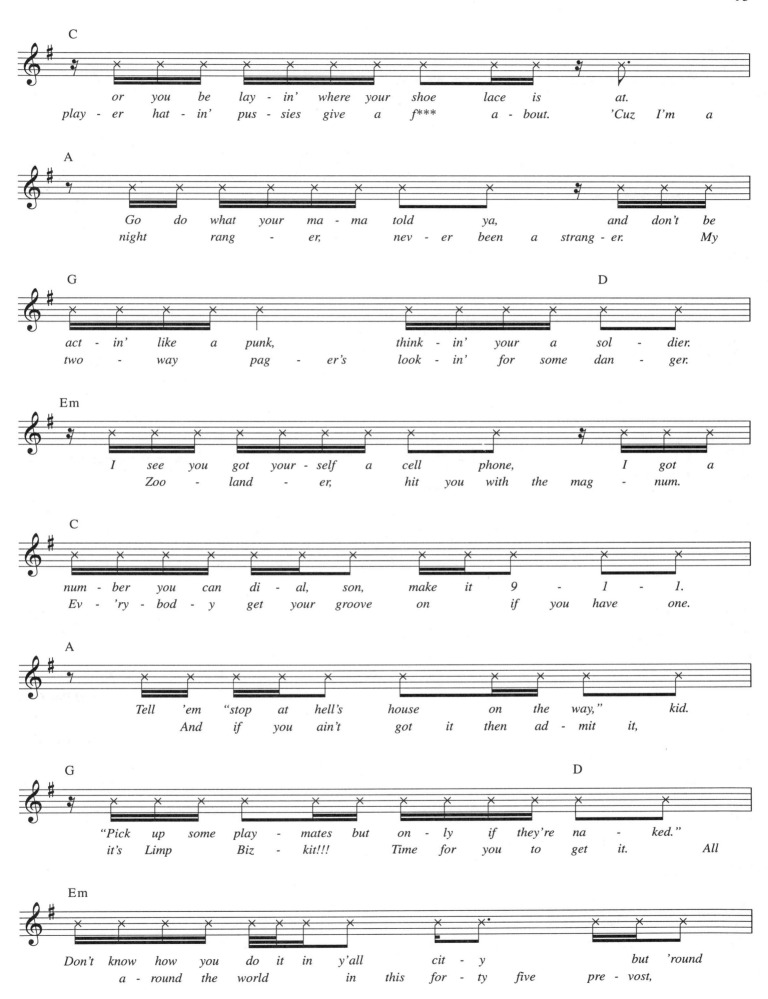

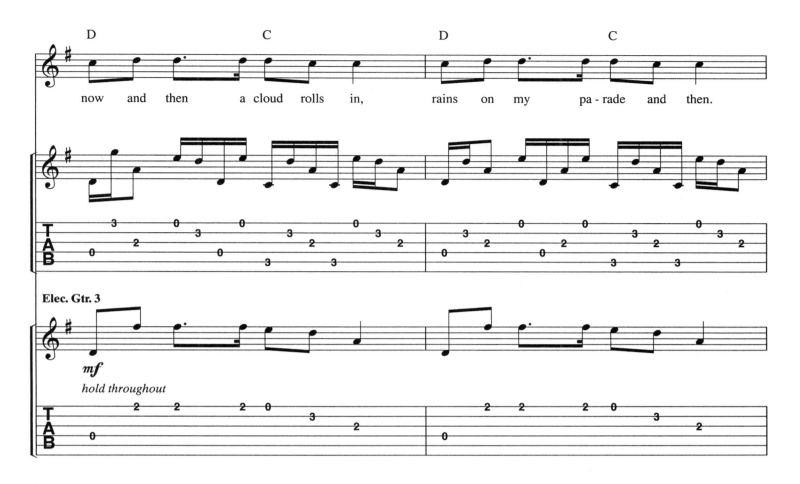

now and then a cloud rolls in, rains on my pa - rade and then.

Elec. Gtr. 3

mf

hold throughout

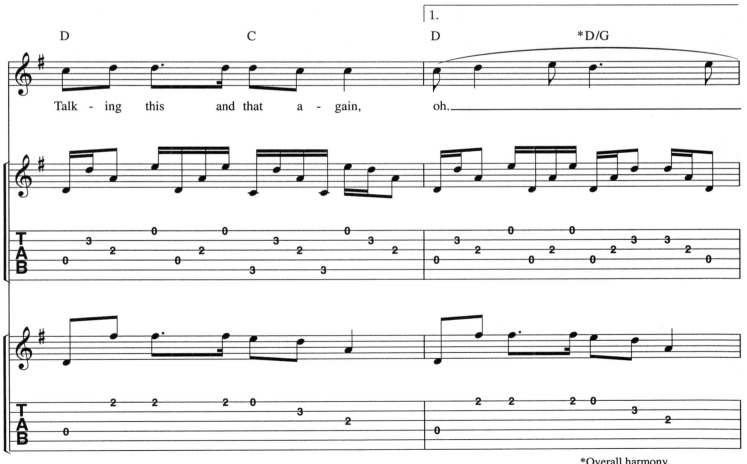

Talk - ing this and that a - gain, oh.

1.

*Overall harmony.

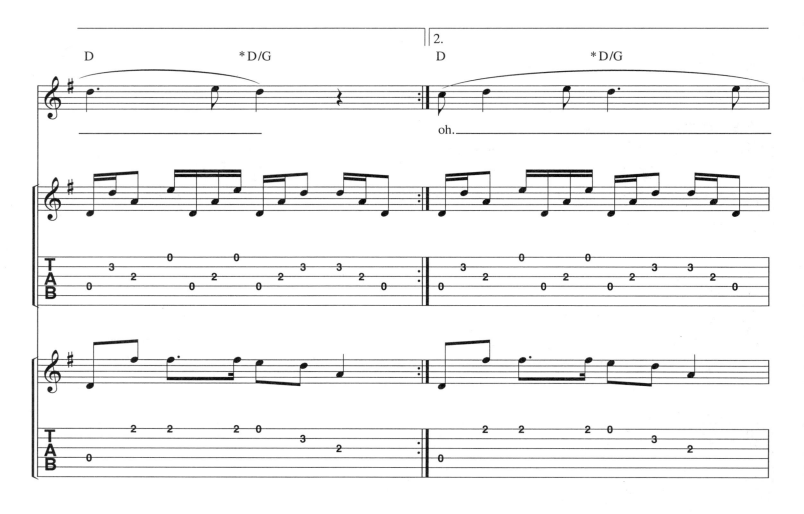

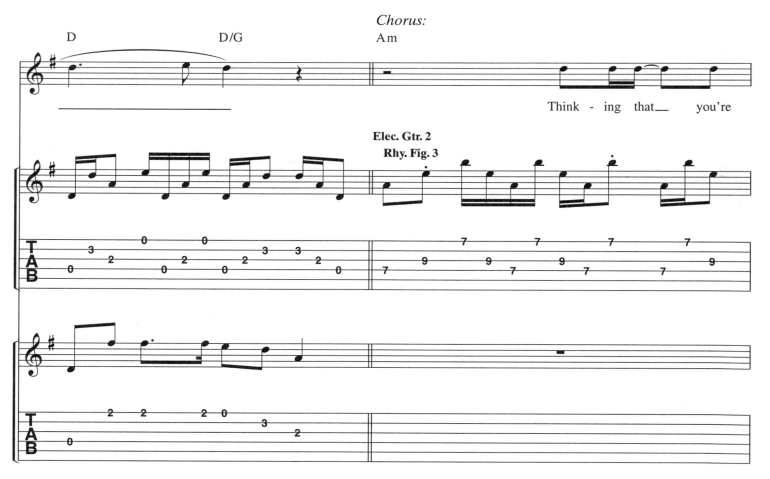

Outro:
w/Rhy. Fig. 1 *(Elec. Gtr. 1) 2 times*

Repeat and fade

Elec. Gtr. 4

Verse 3:
Spoken: *Let me guess, you ain't that impressed,*
Mr. halitosis of the breath.
Livin' life styles of the wish you would,
From the back aisles of the thrifty good.
See I got room to talk, kid,
I've been layin' this track since north cack-a-lack.
And the very first day that you fell out the sack,
I was in some phat laces spinnin' on my back.
Let me think, let me roll, let me ride,
Let me put some funk in the trunk with a vibe.
And a memory that can ease your pain,
Like a melody from Kurt Cobain.
'Cuz ya never know when it's all gonna end,
And ya never know when you call on a friend.
So you better take a step to prepare yourself,
'Cuz the way you're livin' now ain't good for your health.
(To Chorus:)

HEAD FOR THE BARRICADE

Words and Music by
FRED DURST, JOHN OTTO, SAMUEL RIVERS,
MIKE SMITH, MARK MORALES,
DARREN ROBINSON and DAMON YUL WIMBLEY

I'm kind - a sick of be - ing ag - gra - vat - ed. I'm
such a drag___ when there's peo - ple talk - in' down___ to ya.___

glad I'm hat - ed, I guess I'm do - in' some - thing right.
___ Such a drag___ think - ing ev - 'ry - thing sucks._____ (Do ya?)

That's what hap - pened back in Col - um - bine...   you got - ta
...walk a - way___ with the spit on your face?   Or do ya___

know when to stop___ and don't go o - ver the top.   'Cuz there's a
___ draw the line___ just to give 'em a taste?   'Cuz I

cham - ber deep in - side the brain   that's cov - ered with chains,__ so don't be shak - in' 'em loose.__   And if ya
know it's nev - er gon - na end.   If it hap - pens a - gain__ I'm go - ing straight__ for the throat, an - oth - er

do, I'd be run - nin' for the hills   'cuz I'm read - y to rock and now I'm play - in' for real.   }
note, don't for - get you had a chance.   Now I'm off of the side   lines__ and read - y to dance.   }   I got - ta...

You bet - ter watch out   when my a - dren - a - line kicks.   I got - ta...
(Fight!)   (Fight!)

It's too late,   you al - read - y been hit.   Damn.
(Fight!)   (Fight!)

Head for the Barricade - 5 - 2
PGM0323

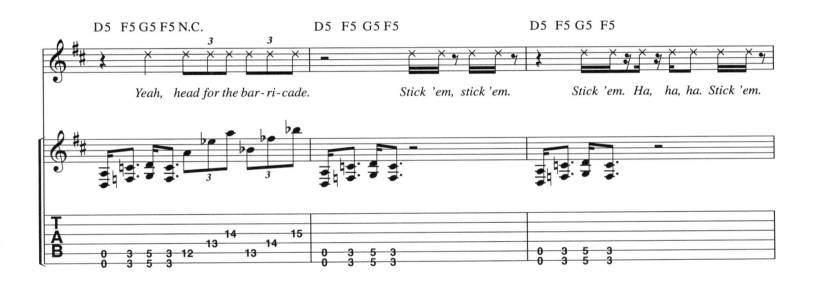

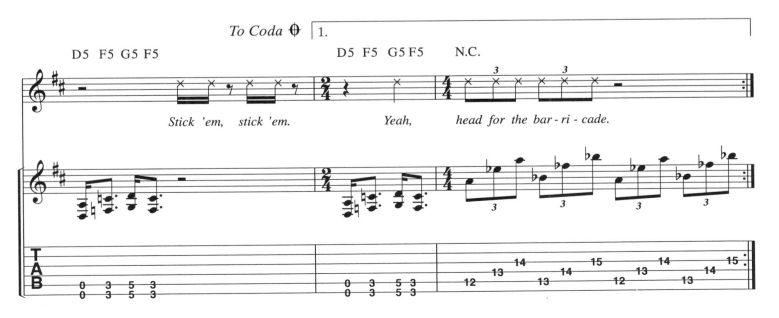

BEHIND BLUE EYES

Words and Music by
PETE TOWNSHEND

Verse 3:

No one knows what it's like to be mistreated,

To be defeated behind blue eyes.

And no one knows how to say that they're sorry,

And don't worry, I'm not telling lies.

(To Chorus:)

DROWN

Words and Music by
FRED DURST and SAMUEL RIVERS

*Recording sounds a minor third lower then written.

**Bass plays E.

Verse:
w/Rhy. Fig. 1 (Elec. Gtr. 1) 2 times

1. It's get-ting clos-er to the end, ev-'ry part of me.
2. It's get-ting clos-er to the end. I look back and smile.

Then dis-as-ter takes its toll and now I'm left with on-ly me.
We con-quered ev-'ry sin-gle bump in my road, made it all worth-while.

Drown - 4 - 1
PGM0323

Drown - 4 - 4
PGM0323

GUITAR TAB GLOSSARY **

TABLATURE EXPLANATION

READING TABLATURE: Tablature illustrates the six strings of the guitar. Notes and chords are indicated by the placement of fret numbers on a given string(s).

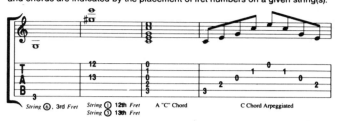

String ⑥, *3rd Fret*   *String* ① *12th Fret*   A "C" Chord   C Chord Arpeggiated
String ③ *13th Fret*

BENDING NOTES

 **HALF STEP:** Play the note and bend string one half step.*

 **WHOLE STEP:** Play the note and bend string one whole step.

 **WHOLE STEP AND A HALF:** Play the note and bend string a whole step and a half.

 **SLIGHT BEND (Microtone):** Play the note and bend string slightly to the equivalent of half a fret.

 **PREBEND (Ghost Bend):** Bend to the specified note, before the string is picked.

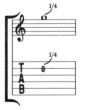 **PREBEND AND RELEASE:** Bend the string, play it, then release to the original note.

 **REVERSE BEND:** Play the already-bent string, then immediately drop it down to the fretted note.

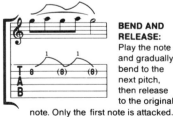 **BEND AND RELEASE:** Play the note and gradually bend to the next pitch, then release to the original note. Only the first note is attacked.

*A half step is the smallest interval in Western music; it is equal to one fret. A whole step equals two frets.

 **UNISON BEND:** Play both notes and immediately bend the lower note to the same pitch as the higher note.

 **DOUBLE NOTE BEND:** Play both notes and immediately bend both strings simultaneously.

 **BENDS INVOLVING MORE THAN ONE STRING:** Play the note and bend string while playing an additional note (or notes) on another string(s). Upon release, relieve pressure from additional note(s), causing original note to sound alone.

 **BENDS INVOLVING STATIONARY NOTES:** Play notes and bend lower pitch, then hold until release begins (indicated at the point where line becomes solid).

TREMOLO BAR

 **SPECIFIED INTERVAL:** The pitch of a note or chord is lowered to a specified interval and then may or may not return to the original pitch. The activity of the tremolo bar is graphically represented by peaks and valleys.

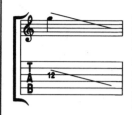 **UN-SPECIFIED INTERVAL:** The pitch of a note or a chord is lowered to an unspecified interval.

HARMONICS

 **NATURAL HARMONIC:** A finger of the fret hand lightly touches the note or notes indicated in the tab and is played by the pick hand.

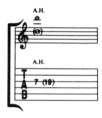 **ARTIFICIAL HARMONIC:** The first tab number is fretted, then the pick hand produces the harmonic by using a finger to lightly touch the same string at the second tab number (in parenthesis) and is then picked by another finger.

 **ARTIFICIAL "PINCH" HAR-MONIC:** A note is fretted as indicated by the tab, then the pick hand produces the harmonic by squeezing the pick firmly while using the tip of the index finger in the pick attack. If parenthesis are found around the fretted note, it does not sound. No parenthesis means both the fretted note and A.H. are heard simultaneously.

© 1990 Beam Me Up Music
c/o CPP/Belwin, Inc. Miami, Florida 33014
International Copyright Secured   Made in U.S.A.   All Rights Reserved

**By Kenn Chipkin and Aaron Stang

RHYTHM SLASHES

STRUM INDICA-TIONS: Strum with indicated rhythm.

The chord voicings are found on the first page of the transcription underneath the song title.

INDICATING SINGLE NOTES USING RHYTHM SLASHES: Very often single notes are incorporated into a rhythm part. The note name is indicated above the rhythm slash with a fret number and a string indication.

ARTICULATIONS

HAMMER ON: Play lower note, then "hammer on" to higher note with another finger. Only the first note is attacked.

LEFT HAND HAMMER: Hammer on the first note played on each string with the left hand.

PULL OFF: Play higher note, then "pull off" to lower note with another finger. Only the first note is attacked.

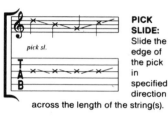

FRET-BOARD TAPPING: "Tap" onto the note indicated by + with a finger of the pick hand, then pull off to the following note held by the fret hand.

TAP SLIDE: Same as fretboard tapping, but the tapped note is slid randomly up the fretboard, then pulled off to the following note.

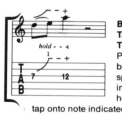

BEND AND TAP TECHNIQUE: Play note and bend to specified interval. While holding bend, tap onto note indicated.

LEGATO SLIDE: Play note and slide to the following note. (Only first note is attacked).

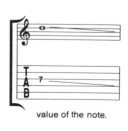

LONG GLISSAN-DO: Play note and slide in specified direction for the full value of the note.

SHORT GLISSAN-DO: Play note for its full value and slide in specified direction at the last possible moment.

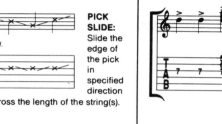

PICK SLIDE: Slide the edge of the pick in specified direction across the length of the string(s).

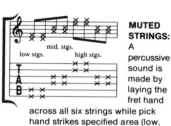

MUTED STRINGS: A percussive sound is made by laying the fret hand across all six strings while pick hand strikes specified area (low, mid, high strings).

PALM MUTE: The note or notes are muted by the palm of the pick hand by lightly touching the string(s) near the bridge.

TREMOLO PICKING: The note or notes are picked as fast as possible.

TRILL: Hammer on and pull off consecutively and as fast as possible between the original note and the grace note.

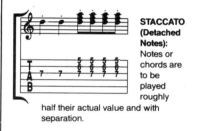

ACCENT: Notes or chords are to be played with added emphasis.

STACCATO (Detached Notes): Notes or chords are to be played roughly half their actual value and with separation.

DOWN STROKES AND UPSTROKES: Notes or chords are to be played with either a downstroke (⊓) or upstroke (∨) of the pick.

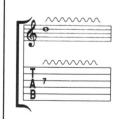

VIBRATO: The pitch of a note is varied by a rapid shaking of the fret hand finger, wrist, and forearm.